T0095414

The Baptism of the Holy Spirit

The Baptism of the Holy Spirit

Simple Answers for Seekers

Don Hightower

THE BAPTISM OF THE HOLY SPIRIT
SIMPLE ANSWERS FOR SEEKERS

Scripture taken from the HOLY BIBLE, NEW INTERNATIONAL VERSION. Copyright 1973, 1978, 1984 by International Bible Society. Used by permission of Zondervan. All rights reserved.

iUniverse books may be ordered through booksellers or by contacting:

iUniverse
1663 Liberty Drive
Bloomington, IN 47403
www.iuniverse.com
1-800-Authors (1-800-288-4677)

ISBN: 978-1-4917-6538-8 (sc)
ISBN: 978-1-4917-6539-5 (e)

Library of Congress Control Number: 2015905899

Print information available on the last page.

iUniverse rev. date: 04/28/2015

Contents

A little background music please ...

The doctrine of the Holy Spirit is a very involved study if one is going to cover the whole subject from Genesis to Revelation. However, we will leave the longer studies to the theologians, for we simply want to cover the teachings of the Holy Spirit for the believer today, and more specifically, the baptism of the Spirit. I should have written this booklet many years ago because there is such a need for it. There has always been, except for the first 300 years or so of the new church age, when they knew and experienced the things of the Spirit more than we do today. There is such a great misunderstanding of the Holy Spirit and what the believer is supposed to expect or experience or "feel" or do. The early church learned from Jesus about the wonderful truths of the Spirit. Then as the decades and few centuries went by and the precious truths began to fall to the practices of men, the believers struggled on their own power for centuries and often fell into darkness and unneeded wanderings. From my studies in early church history, I found that probably the first major teaching to be dropped from the church was the teaching and belief in the baptism of the Holy Spirit and the accompanying gifts of the Spirit, which left the church rather powerless, unlike the first-century church of Peter and Paul. There are, however, many reports down through church history of the Holy Spirit breaking out among some people here and there with the accompanying praying in tongues, healings, and the gifts of the Spirit. It never completely died out, especially among those few believers who wanted more than just church. Where the Spirit was sought, there could usually be found the outward evidence in many ways, much like today. Those who seek will find.

But God cannot leave his people alone. Near the end of the 19th century there were reports that searching Christians were finding new, no old, experiences of healings, miracles, the baptism of the Spirit, the gifts of the Spirit being manifested, and many other signs that God's promises were still here. Then as the powerful Azuza Street revival hit Los Angeles, it was obvious to much of the Christian world, that something big was happening even though many denominations and churches did their best to ignore since it wasn't in their doctrinal statement. That is the test you know! The Christian world looked upon it as a "fanatical" thing and not much more. However the spiritual world was being shaken and churches and teachings were being established that made Christians all over the world realize things were never going to be the same again. And later, in the late 1960s and all of the 1970s, came another wave, often called the charismatic outpouring, that hit the church and the world with its power. I was a part of that wave. And I was never the same after that, in a good way, in case you are wondering.

I was hungry anyway as a Christian and a pastor at that time. I often prayed that God would give me more. I would even hear very quietly the whispering of God as he would speak to me inwardly and say, "There is more; there is more." I knew that, at least, I wanted that and hoped that, but I didn't know what that "more" was. I received the baptism of the Holy Spirit in a scriptural way, and not long after that, as I was reading in I Corinthians 14 about the gifts of the Spirit, where it said to earnestly desire the gifts, especially the gift of prophecy (in verse 1), I just stopped and prayed and said, "God, I don't know much about these gifts" (and I am ashamed to say I was a pastor too), "but if it is your will, would you give me any of these gifts especially the gift of prophecy like your word says?" I was very serious about this. In about 45 minutes I started having the first vision that I ever had, though since then I have had many visions, which are a common way for God to reveal things to me. It was a clear vision about a family member of ours and an event that was happening in the vision. It lasted maybe 20 seconds at the most but it was very clear, and seemed certain to be a warning of something that was not good that was going to happen to this person. So my wife and I kept it in our hearts and prayed about the person for quite awhile. Finally, about 2 ½ years later we got a call from that family about a medical problem. Things developed quickly and all of a sudden, my wife and I realized that the vision I had seen was in progress, not quite in the way that we thought, but it all worked out for good. See Rom. 8:28. It actually took many years for the last detail to come to pass, but God finished it all to his glory! In the meantime, though, God had been putting some of his gifts of the Spirit within me and I was learning how they worked as my faith grew by leaps and bounds. It soon became obvious that the Lord was calling me into more of a prophetic ministry and combining that with my Bible teaching ministry. Large numbers of people around me, in Peoria, Illinois, were also receiving the baptism of the Spirit and we were all learning together, though many of them needed a Bible foundation for additional help. I saw the need for the Holy Spirit in our lives and the difference it makes when the Spirit is not stressed in a church, or worse, ignored, or still worse, fought against. I was relieved of my pastor's license in my denomination because of receiving the baptism of the Spirit. But I went on in my life and allowed God to lead me where he wanted me. I thought that God might call me to Little Rock, Arkansas because I already had friends there and had been invited down "if something happens," they said. But it soon became obvious that I should stay in the Peoria area. It did not take me long to see the huge gap between serving the Lord without the Spirit and serving the Lord with the leading of the Spirit. It is night and day. The two types of lives do not resemble each other. I have been serving the Lord for over 40 years under the leading of the Holy Spirit and I still am amazed that I tried the ways of man for so many years, the intellectual thing, the "white knuckle club" as Bob Mumford used to call it. You know, where YOU have to think everything through and figure out how YOU will solve this problem and how YOU will push this in church, or how YOU will get a prayer answered. I was my own strength then, but not now. I was my own wisdom, but not now. Yep, most Christians serve the Lord through their soul, not their spirit. In fact, most Christians don't even know the difference between their soul and spirit. Pastors are not teaching anything about the Holy Spirit unless it is a few minor things. They know very little about the power. The baptism of the Spirit makes that difference.

As I look at the American church today, I wonder how much longer God will let us keep going on our own powerless selves, pushing man's programs, trying new things to get some kind of life in the church. The average Christian's life is dryer than last week's popcorn. I see people pushing themselves to go to church, forcing themselves to read a few Bible verses or to pray a little. It is because of this, that I wrote this booklet. I want to pour water on your thirst. I want to see joy in your life. I pray that you will snap the chains off, that you will begin to grow in faith like never before, that life and miracles will take place within you and all around you and your family and church. The Holy Spirit is a very big key to that. A very big key. If you will open your Bibles and your hearts to what God has for you, you will never thirst again. John 4:14.

CHAPTER 1

The early promises of the Holy Spirit

How God loves his people! He has always given his people blessings and life that they never deserved and he has always had them to look ahead, also, to the blessings and life that he had for them in their next step of the eternal ages. God's requirements for Israel were rather easy – just keep the law and do good. Keep the holy days, remember the sacrifices, treat your neighbor well, and stay within the boundaries. It seems rather simple to me, a Gentile and someone who never was under the law of Moses. But, more than that, it looked as if there was something missing in the law, and that was life -- joyful, expectant, hopeful life. The biggest change, spiritually, in Israel was when they returned from captivity in Babylon. God had told them that he was going to do something different in their nation, and he did, and it had to do with the Holy Spirit. Whenever the Holy Spirit moves into the picture, there is always change.

Ezekiel was in Babylon, rebuking, correcting, and encouraging them at the time. Early in his writings, in chapter 11, he said that God was going to bring them out of Babylon and return them to their land. Then he said in verse 19, "I will give them an undivided heart and put a new spirit in them; I will remove from them their heart of stone and give them a heart of flesh." God was going to do something new in Israel. He was a little more specific in Ezk. 36:26, 27 where he promised: "I will give you a new heart and put a new spirit in you; I will remove from you your heart of stone and give you a heart of flesh. And I will put my Spirit in you and move you to follow my decrees and be careful to keep my laws." Up until this time the Holy Spirit had not lived within God's people, but only "around" them in various degrees. We do see a few people, like Bezalel, who helped build the tabernacle and was so skilled in his work that God said about him that he was "filled with the Spirit." See Ex. 31:3. This does not mean the same as in the New Testament or for today, but meant that God used his Spirit to guide this man in his special work. Usually we see that the Spirit "came down" upon the prophets when they prophesied or the Lord did a miracle through someone. It was temporary and for a specific purpose.

But God started giving Israel promises that the Holy Spirit was coming in a different way. Ezekiel gave more of these promises that the Holy Spirit was going to be "in" people, not just around them or something temporary. In 37:14 he said, "I will put my Spirit in you and you will live, and I will settle you in your own land. Then you will know that I the Lord have spoken, and I have done it, declares the Lord." Years earlier Isaiah had promised similar things in 44:3. "For I will pour water on the thirsty land, and streams on the dry ground; I will pour out my Spirit on your offspring and my blessing on your descendants."

God also made sure that Israel, and all of God's people that were aware of it, would find promises more for the last days that would explode with the power of the Spirit and would be signs for the whole world to see. As Ezekiel described the giant war that was coming with Gog and Magog, in chapter 38 and 39, he encouraged them with another promise of the coming Holy Spirit in verse 29: "I will no longer hide my face from them, for I will pour out my Spirit on the house of Israel, declares the Sovereign Lord." Isaiah foretold of Israel's coming judgment followed with mercy and blessings. He said in 32:15 that the Spirit would be "poured" upon them from on high. The terms "poured out" or "poured upon" shows a powerful rainstorm of the Holy Spirit upon a people without regard to age, gender, location, even spiritual condition.

This is exactly what the prophet Joel was stressing in the famous passage in 2:28-32. Peter quotes this whole passage in Acts 2 on the day of Pentecost to show the people that this scripture was being partially fulfilled. God said in Joel 2:28, 29, "And afterward, I will pour out my Spirit on all people. Your sons and daughters will prophesy, your old men will dream dreams, your young men will see visions. Even on my servants, both men and women, I will pour out my Spirit in those days." This was a unique prophecy. No one had ever said this before in all of the Old Testament. Plus, it was so pointed in that it tells of young people and old people getting prophesies and dreams and visions, something unheard of. It sounds as if the revelation of the Lord was going to become common among the people, that is, it was not going to be confined to just the "religious" priests or leaders.

In verses 30, 31, the prophecy shows that it was going to bring forth atmospheric and geophysical signs to masses of people and it would be "before the coming of the great and dreadful day of the Lord." So this is an end-time prophecy. As I said in the last paragraph, Peter quotes this to show that the words were starting to be fulfilled in his day, especially the outpouring of the Spirit, and the rest would be fulfilled in God's timetable.

Then the prophecy finishes on a very high note as it shows that this day will be a great day of salvation as "everyone who calls on the name of the Lord will be saved." Probably the people of Israel thought that these promises would most likely be fulfilled in the new age, not in this age. Like believers today, they probably reserved too much for eternity and not nearly enough for the battles of today. God, however, was preparing Israel, and all others who would believe, for a glorious life, for the here and now, filled with power and wonders and experiences that were beyond words. God always prepares us, gives us glimpses of our future, gets our faith built up so that we can receive. That is what most of the Bible is all about. We all know that eternity will be wonderful but not many are filled with a similar excitement for today. That is why God prepared Israel, told them of marvelous things to come, and got them ready for a whole new age, the age of the Holy Spirit.

CHAPTER 2

Along comes Jesus

It had been a long silence. Over 400 years had passed since a prophet had brought any kind of hope to Israel or the surrounding nations. Lots of changes had taken place during those dark years. Israel had almost been wiped out as a nation by the most wicked Antiochus Epiphanes, a type of the antichrist, and his Syrian army. But God had his heroes ready and they came through to win the Maccabean War. Soon after Rome conquered the whole territory and now Israel was under a slightly more compassionate law but it was still an iron hand. The Pharisees and Sadducees had arisen in power during this time and added so many hundreds of man-made laws to the original Law of Moses that the people were now slaves to the religious leaders. The people were under a firm foreign law and a national religious law and many of them had given up on ever seeing the promised Messiah.

"But when the time had fully come, God sent his Son, born of a woman, born under law to redeem those under law, that we might receive the full rights of sons. Because you are sons, God sent the Spirit of his Son into our hearts." Galatians 4:4-6.

Jesus had a tremendous amount of work to do in his three and one-half year ministry. He had to show the people who he was, heal them, deliver them, teach them, pick out 12 disciples, teach them who he was, teach them that he was going to die, be raised from the dead, ascend to heaven and leave them here, pour out his Spirit on all believers, and then return one day. He was a Bible school on the move.

Jesus was bringing in the age of grace, or the age of salvation, or the age of the Holy Spirit. These new, powerful blessings were going to be offered not only to Israel, but to all the Gentiles, all who would believe. Isaiah told of this many times in the latter part of his book.

The Master Teacher did not waste time in revealing the things that the Father wanted to do in the people, even the mysterious things of the Holy Spirit. Even before Jesus was beginning to be known, or had started teaching, or had offered himself as the perfect sacrifice, the promises of the Holy Spirit were given. I believe that God wanted Israel to become curious, even hungry, for what this Jesus was going to do. God started laying down promises of a "baptism of the Holy Spirit." When John the Baptizer started his preaching he announced clearly to the people that he was only baptizing in water for repentance' sake, then he added, "But after me will come one who is more powerful than I, whose sandals I am not fit to carry. He will baptize you with the Holy Spirit and with fire." Mt. 3:11. This was so important for us to know that God repeated it in all 4 Gospels. See Mk. 1:8 and Lk. 3:16. But John says it even better. In his first chapter, John the Baptizer saw

Jesus coming and announced to the ones around him that this was the Lamb of God who would take away the sins of the world. Jn. 1:29. Then John says that he would not have known this except that God told him ahead of time that when he would see the Holy Spirit come down, in the form of a dove, and land on a man, that would be the Messiah, and this one would be the one who "baptizes" with the Holy Spirit. See v. 33. The New International Version and some other translations have it wrong and say that Jesus is the one who "will baptize with the Holy Spirit." But it is "baptizes," a continual process coming from Jesus, he will keep on baptizing people with the Spirit, just as he will keep on saving and healing and doing all of his other wonderful works. Jesus is the baptizer, not man, or churches, or organizations. He does it and everything that Jesus and the apostles did in the New Testament is for us today. None of the promises have become useless, or powerless, or outdated or anything else that the excusers say.

When the people of Israel heard John say that someone was going to "baptize" them in the Holy Spirit, they were not altogether ignorant of this word. Way back in the law of Moses (Lev. 15 and 17:15, 16) there were numerous cleansing rituals with water which were done to show that a person was physically and spiritually clean and free of something. That word "baptism" was used a few times in the Septuagint, a Greek translation of the Jewish scriptures, and Greek was a language that the people of Jesus' time understood. By the time the Essenes came along, a few generations before Jesus, they were practicing a more definite baptism which showed a whole spiritual cleansing in the person's life. It is believed that the Essenes wrote most or all of the Dead Sea Scrolls and in there, the rite was given to those who wanted to completely be purified and to avoid a coming visitation or judgment upon the ungodly of Israel. So a water baptism was in practice by the time of John the baptizer, only John now emphasized repentance as a requirement for receiving it. He was baptizing in the Jordan River, immersing the people and proclaiming their new walk in life, so his visual aid was a perfect setting to announce a new kind of baptism, a baptism in the Holy Spirit, which to the people would indicate a complete immersion in Spirit.

Jesus continued to teach the people about the Spirit, especially as he got closer to the time of his death. The new birth would be powerless to change a life unless the convert drinks in all of the Spirit. One of the big reasons that so many Christians get discouraged about their walk with the Lord is that the church has failed to teach them about the power that is ours through the Holy Spirit. They have been cheated out of a large part of the gospel. They struggle with many things and sometimes drop out, all because they never heard anything about the baptism of the Holy Spirit.

John, the more internal and spiritual of the 4 Gospels, has more to say on the coming Spirit than the other 3, although Luke does make a startling promise, in 11:13, where he assures them that the Father will give the Holy Spirit to those who ask. God will just "give" it to them? You surely have to do more than just ask; that is far too simple. But the promise is true, although there are a few requirements, for example, a person has to be "born again" as Jesus started teaching in Jn. 3:1-8, and a person has to know something about this gift and has to want it. You cannot simply "try it." Too many people have done that and lost what little joy they had about the things of God. You have to have at least enough faith to receive, which is not a difficult thing at all. Believing is not hard. It is natural with a Christian.

Jesus was at the Feast of Tabernacles (Jn. 7:37-39) together with a large crowd and stood up and proclaimed: "If anyone is thirsty, let him come to me and drink. Whoever believes in me, as the Scripture has said, streams of living water will flow from within him." John explains it by saying: "By this he meant the Spirit, whom those who believed in him were later to receive. Up to that time the Spirit had not been given, since Jesus had not yet been glorified." This scripture was partially fulfilled at the Day of Pentecost and gets fulfilled again every time someone receives the baptism of the Holy Spirit. Jesus said that he was going to give the Spirit to all people and they could drink all they wanted and a supernatural thing would happen. Streams of living water would flow from within him, the believer, to whatever need that had to be met or whatever purpose God had. These streams are new languages that God gives a person when they receive. Not one new language, but many. More on this later.

John gives several key promises about the Spirit in the latter half of his book. He tells the disciples a new thing when he tells them that he was going to send a Counselor, the Spirit of truth. Then Jesus says, "The world cannot accept him because it neither sees him nor knows him. But you know him, for he lives WITH you and will be IN you." Jn. 14:16,17. God had never done this before. Of all the good people and servants of God that had come before them, no one had experienced the Holy Spirit living permanently inside of them. But this was going to happen to all those who wanted those promises. This new age that was soon coming was going to be the age of the Holy Spirit, where the Spirit dwelled inside of every believer and they could choose the depth of the life that they wanted in the Spirit.

Jesus still did not give a lot of details about what was going to happen to him after he was raised from the dead. That was a lot for the disciples to absorb. They had not even accepted his several statements about his soon-coming death. But he gave pieces of information about their future and they quickly began to put it all together after they had witnessed his resurrection. After he was raised he met with them, in Jn. 20:19-23, and did a rather strange thing. He said that he was sending them out (to later preach the gospel) and then he breathed on them and said, "Receive the Holy Spirit." This was similar to God breathing into the lifeless clay body of Adam and Adam coming alive in the creation story. Gen. 2:7. Now, Jesus was breathing into the disciples the new creation. II Cor. 5:17. Most Bible teachers say that this was the initial and visible giving of the Holy Spirit to the disciples, but was also a demonstration for them to see that all believers from then on would be indwelt by the Spirit. The Bible shows that all true believers in Christ "have" the Holy Spirit. In fact, Paul says if you do not have the Spirit of Christ, you do not belong to Christ. See Rom. 8:9.

So now that Jesus had been raised from the dead and proven that he was the Promised One, he could give out his Spirit to all who chose him. This was not the baptism of the Holy Spirit into which we are looking, but was the Spirit being given to all believers. Not all believers have the baptism of the Spirit. It does not come automatically with salvation, in spite of what you may have been taught. To show that, we look at the other words Jesus gave to the disciples at the same night, the first evening of his resurrection. Luke adds more to John's account of that meeting. After telling them that they would go out and preach, he cautions them with: "I am going to send you what my Father has promised; but stay in the city until you have been clothed with power from on high." Lk. 24:49. Do you see that? The disciples have already been given the Holy Spirit when Jesus breathed on them, but Jesus said, "You need more, so wait in the city and you will be given extra power." (My words.) It never hurts to have more of God. I have never heard of anyone who has overdosed.

About 40 days later after Jesus had told these things to them, and teaching them more each day, he has one last time of instruction and fellowship. This was on the day of his ascension. He said again to wait in the city and then added, "For John baptized with water but in a few days you will be baptized with the Holy Spirit." Acts 1:5. The reason for the baptism was given by Jesus in verse 8, where he said, "You will receive power when the Holy Spirit comes on you; and you will be my witnesses in Jerusalem, and in all Judea and Samaria, and to the ends of the earth." The main reason for the gift of the Holy Spirit is to give power for witnessing to other people and the nations. To do the tremendous task of reaching the world with the good news of Christ takes a supernatural amount of power. The Greek word for "power" here is where we get our word for dynamite. The Holy Spirit is dynamite in a person's life when they receive.

So the disciples went to a meeting place and prayed and waited for these promises. That happened 10 days later on the Day of Pentecost, in Acts 2.

Chapter 3

Jesus goes up and the Spirit comes down

We see that after the promise in Acts 1:5, Jesus instructed the disciples a little more and then ascended into heaven in their view. Then they obeyed their Master and stayed all together in Jerusalem for the next 10 days, praising God and anticipating what Jesus was going to do next. It "just happened" that it was a big holiday for the Jews, which was the Day of Pentecost, and thousands of extra Jews were gathered in the city. The disciples had been praying and seeking God when the events of Acts 2 happened. A strong wind from heaven came down, as well as "tongues of fire" that lit on each of them. Then v. 4 is what we are looking at. It says, "All of them were filled with the Holy Spirit and began to speak in other tongues as the Spirit enabled them." When it says "all of them," we do not know for sure if that means the whole 120 of them mentioned in 1:15 or just the 12 disciples. More scholars agree that it probably means all 120 received this experience. I counted 15 nationalities and languages named in Acts 2 where the people spoke out about hearing the different tongues. So probably all 120 of the gathered people were rejoicing and speaking in a new tongue. Notice that all of them did receive, not just some of them or a few of them. Notice that tongues seemed to be the evidence here that something supernatural had happened to each of them. Lastly, notice that this must have been the baptism of the Holy Spirit because Jesus had said 10 days earlier in 1:5 that they would be baptized with the Holy Spirit. Many of the disciples and perhaps some others of the group must have spoken supernaturally by the wording here: "began to speak in other tongues as the Spirit enabled them," and by the fact that the foreigners in the crowd heard them speaking in their own native languages. Sometimes when a person receives the baptism of the Spirit, they do speak a foreign, or known language, although it is unknown, or unlearned by the speaker. At other times the tongues will not be recognized and may be a dead language, such as Sanskrit, or even an angelic language as Paul says in I Cor. 13:1. Now through the rest of the Book of Acts there are other instances of people receiving the baptism of the Spirit and it will always be similar to this experience in Acts 2.

Let us go to another instance of the new believers receiving. There are 4 places in Acts where people receive. We have just seen the first one, but we will skip the second instance for now and go to the third instance. The reason for skipping it will be seen later.

For the third instance let us go to Acts 10 where Peter was supernaturally called by God to go speak to the Gentile Cornelius and his household and servants. Peter started preaching the gospel and before he was done, the "Holy Spirit came on all who heard the message. The circumcised believers (the Jews) who had come with Peter were astonished that the gift of the Holy Spirit had been poured out even on the Gentiles for they heard them speaking in tongues and praising God." Acts 10:45, 46. We see very similar facts here that correspond to Acts 2. First, all of them, not just a few, received the baptism of the Spirit. Peter calls it that in 11:15-17. Notice how the Jewish believers there knew that the Gentiles had received the Spirit. It says, "For (or because) they heard them speaking in tongues." This was the same evidence as in Acts 2. This was a turning point in Peter's ministry, and the Jews also, because now they saw that God wanted the Gentiles saved and baptized in the Spirit. A person cannot receive the baptism unless he is saved. So they were saved and baptized in the Spirit all at once. Sometimes that happens, although it is more common to receive the baptism of the Spirit sometime after salvation, whether a week later or years later. It would be far better if people would get saved and baptized in the Spirit at the same time, plus get delivered of demons too. The church of today should be like the New Testament Church and be a "full service church" where people get the whole thing and keep getting more all their life. But today the church gives a little salvation, maybe, and that is it. A little dab'll do ya.

Another interesting thing about this event in chapter 10 is that after the Gentiles got saved and filled, Peter said to get them baptized in water in the name of Jesus Christ, the normal New Testament way. All water baptisms were done that way. Their water baptism is a little problem for some Christians who teach that you have to be baptized in order to be saved, but these people were saved first, then baptized.

That always makes me think of a story by John Poole, an early evangelist. He was having Pentecostal meetings and in came a woman all painted up with makeup and dressed up like a dancer. She came down to the altar to get saved and

John said that "before we could get over there and explain the rules, she got saved." We need to let God be God and we remain as disciples who are always learning.

The fourth place in Acts where a group of people were baptized in the Spirit is in Acts 19:1-7. Paul had met about 12 disciples. We do not know if these people were disciples of John the Baptist who had a limited understanding of Jesus, or if they were disciples of Jesus with a limited understanding. They were believers in Jesus because Paul calls them that in v. 2. But as he was talking to them he knew that something was missing in their lives, so he asked them if they had "received the Holy Spirit" when they believed. Paul meant the baptism of the Spirit. When they said they did not even know about the Holy Spirit, Paul taught them some more and since they had only been baptized in John's baptism, he baptized them in water in Jesus' name, the way that it was done in the New Testament. It says then that when Paul laid his hands on them, "the Holy Spirit came on them, and they spoke in tongues and prophesied. There were about 12 men in all." The same pattern follows Acts 2. When the Holy Spirit came on them, they spoke in tongues. It says there were about 12 men, which assumes that all 12 received. Now there was prophesying also, which is 1 of the 9 gifts of the Spirit named in I Cor. 12:8-10. This is not a sign of the baptism of the Spirit, but a gift of the Spirit, which manifested at that time. There is only 1 evidence for the baptism of the Spirit and that is speaking in tongues. I know people really fight this, but it is true. You may try to circumvent tongues and receive the baptism, but you won't have the real thing.

Prophesying or some other miraculous thing happens once in a while today when someone receives. We have seen and heard of a few people who were so filled with the Spirit at their time of salvation or water baptism that they began to speak in tongues then and sometimes prophesy. The gifts of the Spirit usually follow the baptism, sometimes soon after and sometimes later. But the main thing that we see here is the same pattern as Acts 2 at Pentecost. All people received and all spoke in tongues as evidence of receiving the Holy Spirit.

The last incidence we will go to is in Acts 8:4-24. This is the second time, chronologically, in Acts where people received, but we are going back to it to show some points that are in the same pattern as the other 3 instances.

Philip went to Samaria and preached the good news in power and clarity. The people repented and believed and great signs followed their faith. It says, "With shrieks, evil spirits came out of many, and many paralytics and cripples were healed." Verse 7. There was a man there, Simon, who had been a sorcerer, but was saved and baptized in water like many people there, and it points out that Simon was astonished by the great signs and miracles he saw, in v. 13.

Now an interesting thing happened. The apostles in Jerusalem sent Peter and John to Samaria to help the new believers receive the Holy Spirit. We have seen earlier that all believers "have" the Holy Spirit within them, helping them in their walk with Jesus. But this was again, more than that. It says in v. 16 that "the Holy Spirit had not yet come upon any of them; they had simply been baptized into the name of the Lord Jesus." In other words, the believers had been baptized in water properly but were not baptized in the Holy Spirit like the disciples were at Pentecost. The disciples were not satisfied, as so many churches and Christians are today, with people getting saved and baptized in water and that is all. No, you can see in this section of my book that the disciples and early church expected all believers to receive the baptism of the Spirit. So Peter and John laid hands on them and they received the Holy Spirit. How did they know they had received the Holy Spirit? Because, it says in v. 18, that Simon "saw" that the Spirit was given at the laying on of the apostles' hands. He saw something tangible, visible, and unique. It was not the demons coming out. He had been a sorcerer; he knew all about demons. He had used demons for years. Nor was it the miracles or healings. He had seen those earlier and was astonished at the power of God. Simon noticed power, that's what he was all about. So what happened at the baptism of the Spirit when these people received? The same as the other times in Acts 2, 10, and 19. These believers spoke in tongues too. That is what Simon "saw." That was a miracle that Simon could not imitate. If that is not what happened, what was it? God's word is consistent. It was the same evidence as before. Peter did have to correct Simon about his offer to pay money for the gift of laying hands on people for them to get the Spirit, and Simon did repent.

So there is a clear pattern in the book of Acts that God has given us for the baptism of the Spirit. The people prayed or had hands laid on them and they got the Spirit. The evidence was speaking in tongues as God gave them the ability to do that. It was instant, not learned, and was consistent throughout Acts. All of them received too, not just a few select ones. It was not "spooky" or "weird" or "Satanic" or anything else as it is sometimes called today. It was a normal, universal blessing that followed the plan of God from way back to John the Baptist. I will expand on the teaching of tongues in the next chapter because that is a real hangup to many people who have been taught wrong.

CHAPTER 4

Why would God choose tongues?

Satan has an extreme hatred for the phenomena of tongues. He knows that it can radically change a person, like it did me. When I received, my life took a sharp turn upward as the Bible became far more alive that it ever had, and I thought that I had loved the word. The Spirit opened up my spiritual eyes to many things in the word that I had never seen before. My love for people was immensely increased, my faith jumped by sevenfold, my prayer life became filled with praise and thanksgiving, my sensitivity to God became a whole new thing to me, my preaching and teaching took on a whole new life, everything looked better, I even smelled the flowers that I had never noticed before. Honestly! I had been a Christian for 10 years without the baptism of the Spirit, and now I was beginning to find out what it meant to be led of the Spirit. I had not known before even though I thought I was being led of the Spirit. To many Christians, "things" had been a routine, not a joy, not filled with power and confidence. I say this to tell you why Satan hates the baptism. He never lied to me about my salvation but he immediately lied to me and told me that what I had was not real. It was amazing because it was the first time that I had ever heard "a voice." I believed it for a little while until a friend corrected me and after that, I started living in the Spirit and have never looked back. I have discovered that almost everyone I pray with about receiving the Holy Spirit gets lied to by Satan. He tells them almost the same thing as he told me. He knows that without the Spirit many Christians are limited at the least and often weak and can be easily defeated without the power of God working on their behalf. Remember, Jesus told the disciples to wait in Jerusalem until they had "been clothed with power from on high." Lk. 24:49. They had already received the Spirit when Jesus breathed on them, but they had not received the baptism of the Spirit. And a little later Jesus told them again that they would receive power when the Holy Spirit came upon them, in Acts 1:8. An average Christian is not much of a threat to Satan. I hope that I am not making you angry with these statements, but I am telling you the truth. Just think, Christians are already defeated when they think that the baptism of the Spirit is not for today as so commonly taught. Or when they think that tongues are a lot of gibberish as it is often called. Or when they are confused about it being for only a few Christians, those "Pentecostal people." Or when they are afraid of the Holy Spirit. How can they be led of the Spirit when they are afraid of the Spirit? More mockery has been made about the baptism of the Spirit and tongues than any other Bible doctrine. Why? Because Satan wants to keep people, and especially Christians, confused, weak, and powerless. When a person gets baptized in the Spirit and starts learning how to use their new supernatural language, it does a lot of damage to the kingdom of Satan. The fact that Satan hates it so much shows me how powerful it is.

I have covered enough material to show that the baptism is for everyone (unless a reader is just not going to believe that anyway) and that the evidence of it was speaking in tongues. But why tongues? That is a massive question. But it has some very wise answers coming from the writing of God.

One of the first confusing things that should be settled is a couple of definitions about tongues. This is very important. If you understand what is coming up, you will better understand what Paul is talking about in I Cor. 12 and 14.

When a person back in the New Testament, or even today, receives the baptism of the Spirit, they will receive tongues, as we have pointed out. That is what we call their prayer language. Everyone who receives gets a special language from God that he fits with your life and needs, and it is a language that you can then pray with and praise God and sing in, and be blessed and edified as the word teaches. That is for everyone. It is for you personally and only for a personal, daily use. It is powerful as you learn how to use it. It is a mighty weapon so use it carefully.

However, this is not the "gift of tongues." The gift of tongues is when God prompts you in your spirit to speak out loud to a group, whether at church or a prayer meeting, to give a message in tongues that will be followed by interpretation by you or someone else. That is the gift of tongues. Not very many Christians have that gift. That is why Paul asks in I Cor. 12:30, "Do all speak in tongues?" The answer is implied "no." He is talking about the gifts of the Spirit in that passage. He is not asking if everyone should speak in tongues or not. That is where much confusion takes place. Many non-Spirit-filled Christians argue with that verse and say, "See it shows right here that not everyone should speak in tongues." Yes, but Paul is talking about the gift of tongues, not people's prayer language. All of the 9 gifts of the Spirit in I Cor., 12-14 are given only to those people whom God selects.

I received the baptism over 40 years ago and I pray in tongues every day, much of the day, and sing in tongues and praise God in tongues. I believe my spirit is praying in tongues at night while I sleep too. I wake up speaking in tongues many mornings. Our spirit never sleeps, it just keeps praising God if you have opened it up to the fullness of the Lord. However, I have only once spoken in tongues at a prayer meeting with an interpretation that followed. Only once. I do not tell people that I have the gift of tongues because that is not one of my gifts of the Spirit. I have experienced all of the gifts, but some more than others. God uses me to give prophecies at church or at home, which I write down and share the ones that I know are for others. I am used sometimes in the gift of interpretation and in the word of knowledge. Then when I take someone through demon deliverance, the gift of discerning of spirits is at work.

My wife, Sherry, is used quite often in the gift of tongues. She gives a message in tongues at church or a prayer meeting and sometimes she gives the interpretation or sometimes God has me to give the interpretation. She sometimes gives a prophecy at church too. I do not know why God chooses one or the other, but He is God and I try to let him just do his job. A church that I pastored in Peoria had several gifted people and sometimes we had 6 or 7 messages, tongues or prophecy, and 2 or 3 people would share a vision or dream that God had given them the past week. We probably had

12 or 14 people in that little church that had gifts from God. I encouraged testimonies that glorified God and the use of His gifts.

If you understand the difference between tongues as a prayer language that all people can receive, if they want it, and the gift of tongues, that goes only to those whom God chooses, then you can better understand the New Testament and it can prepare you to receive. In I Cor. 14 Paul sometimes is talking about the personal prayer language that all people get with the baptism, and sometimes he is talking about the gift of tongues where only God-selected people speak out loud to be followed by interpretation. A person who has the baptism can fairly easily tell the difference in I Cor. 14 between the 2 kinds of tongues. But a person who has not received can be confused in that chapter if he does not understand the difference.

The second thing that I want to clear up is the question about all people receiving the baptism. I know we covered that a little in the Book of Acts, but I want to give more practical answers here.

The Bible tells us over and over again that God wants to save everyone, but not all people want to be saved. John 3:16, the most famous verse in the Bible, tells us that. Romans 10:9 promises us, "That if you confess with your mouth, 'Jesus is Lord,' and believe in your heart that God raised him from the dead, you will be saved." So simple. It is for everyone. God wants all men to be saved, says I Tim. 2:4.

Just as God wants all sinners to be saved, He wants all Christians to be baptized in the Spirit. Jesus is the only way to salvation and tongues are the only door to the baptism of the Spirit. I am not giving you a pet doctrine of mine, or something that my denomination taught me. Neither, but this is the word of God and it happens to be the way it works out in real life too. My experience matches my doctrine which is a good way to tell if your doctrine is correct. Many people cannot experience their doctrine because it is wrong. So many Christians deny the baptism and say it is not real, just like the Pharisees who tried to deny that Jesus healed the blind man in John 9, but there was the former blind man standing there healed and happy.

For examples on this, I have probably prayed with 150 people or more to receive the baptism and everyone except a few received it and those were the ones who would not open their mouth. They were too embarrassed or too frightened, or could not muster up the faith to speak out because it does take faith to receive, even more faith than getting saved. Every step in my Christian life takes more faith to receive than the previous step. My faith is getting stronger, but the steps are getting bigger. But almost everyone who gets prayer, will receive. All of them should, but a few are kept back by their inhibitions. Many other of my friends tell me the same that all of the people that they pray for receive it, unless they are praying wrong, such as "wait on the Lord, tarry for a few months and you may get it, or get your life straightened out and you can receive." Junk like that never helped anyone. I do not like that old Pentecostal word "tarry." It is a word of doubt, not faith. One of the main reasons why more people haven't received is the wrong way some people pray for them. I did not have anyone around when I got it. I simply went in the church by myself, assumed that I had to speak out somehow, asked God to help me, and I got it. It was a clear, flowing language, like oil coming out of my mouth.

Just to show you how important tongues is to the baptism, I will tell you that you should not only get a language, but the language should develop into a fluent language. The more fluent language that a person has in their life, the more open they will be to other spiritual things. Your spiritual growth in this area will be in proportion to the clarity of your prayer language. I have seen too many Christians that were prayed for and received only a few syllables and that is all they developed, because they had no other instructions, and they eventually lost the enthusiasm for the Spirit and even later denied it because it was not helpful to them. But those who received and developed a clear language went on to other, better things, like receiving some gifts of the Spirit and climbing in their faith.

The language that God gives a person should be a clear, fluent language, although that may not happen immediately until confidence is gained and he learns how to expand his language by faith, just as he first received by faith. The tongue that God gives will be his starting prayer language, but it will enlarge and change and God will add other languages in his life so that his prayers are more versatile and useful. That was what Jesus was talking about in Jn. 7:37-39 where he says: "If anyone is thirsty, let him come to me and drink. Whoever believes in me, as the Scripture has said, streams of living water will flow from within him." Then John adds: "By this he meant the Spirit, whom those who believed in him were later to receive." The wording means that living water will continuously flow out of a person to do whatever God has for his purpose. This is what happens when a person get filled with the Spirit. He will not have just 1 stream of water, but several streams of water, many languages in his daily use. Whatever God wants to speak through him, he will be speaking that language for that day for that purpose. I have 6 or 7 languages in my spiritual tongues. I have an Oriental sounding language when I am doing serious warfare in the heavens. I have a

French sounding, rather smooth, language for praise and communication with God. My main tongue sounds a little like Russian or Scandinavian. Often I hear a word that I think I recognize.

What else does the Bible say about tongues being for all people? On the day that Pentecost happened, Peter preached his famous sermon and said that all people there should repent, be baptized in water and they would receive the gift of the Holy Spirit (the baptism of the Spirit). Then he added, "The promise is for you and your children and for all who are far off – for all whom the Lord our God will call." Acts 2:39. "The promise" of salvation and the Holy Spirit is one promise and is for everyone. When it says, "for all who are far off," it is not talking about ones who are in distant lands, but ones who are far away in time, perhaps generations away. That is to us. It is translated, "to all those in distant times and places."(by C. H. Rieu). R. A. Knox has it, "for all those, however far away, whom the Lord our God calls to himself." The New Living Translation says that it means the Gentiles.

Paul said in I Cor. 14:5: "I would like every one of you to speak in tongues," which shows that not all did, but Paul wished they would, especially if used properly.

I see many reasons why God, in his great wisdom, chose tongues to be such an unusual opening and uplifting boost in the Christian's life. I want to list some of the ways that God uses the blessing of tongues in the lives of those who have received. You may know more reasons than the ones I list, but this is my book, not yours.

The first reason, and the most important reason we speak in tongues, is that we have been commanded to do that. Remember Jesus told the disciples to wait in Jerusalem until they had received power from on high, which he called the baptism of the Spirit. That is in Acts 1:4, 5. If they needed it, why do we not need it? It tells us to "pray in the Spirit" in Eph. 6:18 which means praying in tongues according to Paul who says in I Cor. 14:15 that he prays in the Spirit. The New International Version says, "pray with <u>my</u> spirit" which is not correct. Paul says he prays in the Spirit, sings in the Spirit, and prays with his mind, which is not tongues, just your everyday language. Some people try to say that "praying in the Spirit" is when you get to seriously praying and God takes over and somehow you get to a point where you sense the Spirit. That sounds like something God has to do at his will. It may happen or it may not. No, this is a command that you have to initiate. God would not command us to do something if we can't make it happen on our own. It would be like God telling us to "Perform two miracles each day." You pray in the Spirit and you make it happen. When you pray in tongues or in the Spirit, you do not loose control. You can start or stop any time you want.

Another reason we see it as a command is the clear, short statement of Paul's when he says to "pray continually" in I Thess. 5:17. Does he mean that? Without ever stopping? You know, you cannot possibly do that in English, or your native language, but you can easily fulfill that when you pray in tongues. It is easy and becomes natural to pray in the Spirit all the time without even thinking about it. One of the great miracles about tongues is that it bypasses your tiny little mind and uses your unlimited human spirit. That is why it is called "praying in the Spirit," because it is your spirit praying to and through the Holy Spirit. It is spirit touching Spirit. I could teach a couple of hours on that alone. What a mighty God we serve.

To show more on this phenomena we refer to an experiment that is rather famous among the full gospel people. "When Dr. Andrew Newberg, a neuroscientist, compared brain scans of Christians praying in tongues with Buddhist monks chanting and Catholic nuns praying, the study showed the frontal lobes – the brain's control center – went quiet in the brains of the Christians talking in tongues, proving that speaking in tongues isn't a function of the natural brain but an operation of the Spirit." (70 Reasons for Speaking in Tongues, Bill Hamon; Destiny Image).

Another good reason that God chose tongues to be a channel of blessings is that the Bible says that praying in tongues edifies you. Paul says that in I Cor. 14:4. The word "edifies" means "builds up, strengthens, encourages, emboldens." Jude 20 exhorts us to "build yourselves up in your most holy faith and pray in the Holy Spirit." Praying in tongues certainly does that; it greatly encourages us with supernatural inner strength; it brings joy and hope; it quickly and consistently edifies a person after praying awhile. It is the best depression beater in the world.

Just this one great fact alone, that praying in tongues truly edifies you, should make every Christian want to receive it. Who does not want to feel better? Who does not want to be strengthened by the Lord?

Another reason or use for tongues is found in Romans 8:26. In the few verses before that, Paul tells us that the earth and whole creation literally groans as it waits for the day of redemption. Psalm 19:1, 2 says that the heavens and skies declare the glory of God and "they pour forth speech." Now we do not know what the earth is saying in its groans, or what the heavens are saying as they glorify God, but God knows and communicates with them continually. Just because we don't understand the language does not mean that it has no purpose or that we should throw it all out. So Paul says, "In the same way, the Spirit helps us in our weakness. We do not know what we ought to pray for, but the Spirit himself intercedes for us with groans that words cannot express." This is exactly describing what a useful tool that tongues can be to us. Many times we do not know how to pray about a situation, so we switch over from English to our prayer language, or tongues, and start praying exactly what God desires. It is the Spirit praying through us with the very answers of God. We are bypassing out puny little brain, with all of its understanding and reasoning, and relying upon the great wisdom of the Holy Spirit. Christians need to rely less on their own understanding (Pro. 3:5) and much more on the speaking and leading of the Holy Spirit.

Another wonderful blessing and use of tongues is that tongues will do exactly what Jesus said the Holy Spirit would do. Before he died he told the disciples that he was going to send another Counselor. He was talking about the coming Holy Spirit and he tells us about it in John 14:15 through 16:33. He told them that the Counselor would reveal things to them that they would not know otherwise, that he would teach them "all things" (all things that are needed for the moment) and remind them of what Jesus told them (14:26) and he would "testify about me," that is, he would be a witness in the hearts of believers and would show them what was right and what was wrong, not always of course, but when God would need to direct them. In 16:13 the Counselor would tell them what is yet to come. These are just a few of the ways the Spirit wants to direct our lives. When we pray in tongues we often hear some of these things as we wait on an interpretation or prophecy or another kind of revelation. This long speech of Jesus in Jn. 14-16 very seldom sees much of it fulfilled in the life of a believer who does not have the fullness of the Spirit, but to those who have received, these events are rather common in their churches. When I get together with friends who walk in the

Spirit, we talk about our experiences and we learn from each other how these things work and we push ourselves to go further in the Lord. Even tonight, while I was typing this book, I stopped and prayed for a little girl and while I was praying I had a question for the Lord. I prayed for an answer and within 40 minutes the phone rang and the Christian lady on the phone answered my question. God wants to help us, guide us, encourage us without measure. I am finding more and more, as we move closer into these last days that God wants to answer our prayers faster and bigger and bring about greater results.

When it comes right down to it, the purpose of a new, supernatural prayer language is to do the work of God, to be a witness wherever he puts you, like it says in Acts 1:8. If miracles of healing or revelation are needed, they are there by the Spirit. If a prophecy is needed because some of God's people are discouraged, God will send it through one of his faithful servants. That is what Paul means when he says in I Cor. 12:31 to "earnestly desire the greater gifts." We are to be open to receiving the spiritual gifts of God listed there and be ready to be used in bringing forth the gift that is needed for the situation. It should not be translated the "higher" gifts or "best" gifts, because that makes them sound like they are ranked and they are not. All are important. God wants us to move in his power like the apostles and Christians did in the New Testament. That is our pattern and it has never been withdrawn.

I will list one more reason for tongues. They are very wonderful in worship. Paul says, in I Cor. 14:15, that we should sing in the Holy Spirit (or sing in the human spirit). Either way is correct in the action because both our spirit and the Holy Spirit are used in the process. Singing in the Spirit is also mentioned in Eph. 5:19 and Col. 3:16 where it tells us to sing "spiritual songs" which means "songs of the Spirit" or "songs from the Spirit." As our church gets to singing and worshiping, we sometimes go into a familiar tune together but using harmonies as we sing in tongues. In a large church you can hear waves of spontaneous harmonies coming from all directions. It is one of the most beautiful expressions you can hear.

Once in a while a skeptical person will ask me why I like to talk about tongues so much. The previous pages are only a few reasons why. By the way, my first love is Jesus, and he is the one I talk about the most, but to get more of Jesus, after you get saved, you need to get baptized in the Holy Spirit and tongues is the avenue to that. A Christian may never get baptized in the Spirit but he will keep himself from getting more of Jesus.

Chapter 5

How to receive the baptism of the Spirit

This chapter should be short and easy because receiving the baptism of the Spirit is easy, but so many people make it difficult, so we will cover a number of areas here.

I have stated earlier in the book that only two things are necessary to receive: you must be a born-again Christian and you have to really want to receive. You cannot just "try it." God knows your heart. If you are serious you can have it. It is a gift, like salvation. If you are waiting for all of your questions to be answered first, before you receive, then you will never receive. You will never do anything if you are waiting for all questions to be answered. You need a positive attitude. Our God is always "yes."

If you can, you should have a person or some people who are also filled with the Spirit to lay hands on you to receive. They should read or quote Acts 2:4 for you, which says, "All of them were filled with the Holy Spirit and began to speak in other tongues as the Spirit enabled them." Notice that they "all" spoke in tongues "as the Spirit enabled them."

They spoke but the Spirit gave the language. They should pray a Biblical prayer for this, asking God to baptize you in the Spirit, and thanking him for giving you a beautiful prayer language. As they are finishing you probably will feel the Spirit moving around your chest area, close to your throat. God is prompting you to speak. You should begin, by faith, to speak out in tongues. It may be a "b" sound or a "r" sound or any other sound, but that is the beginning. It will be a short syllable or two at first, then as you keep speaking it will come in more syllables and sounds. No one should say, "Here is what it sounds like – do bah lubba fammy oh fen garsto" or something like that. I just made up those sounds. Those are not real words that I know of. They should not try to get you to imitate their tongues. No, God has a perfect spiritual language for you. I know this sounds almost impossible, that you are being asked to speak a language that you don't even know how it starts or sounds. After 40 years of praying in tongues, when I start, I never know the first sound or syllable that will come out of my mouth. I just take off and pray and that is what God wants you to do. It is an act of faith each time. You must open your mouth in order to speak. That is a pretty obvious rule. Do not speak in English or confuse yourself by saying "Thank you Jesus" or "Praise you God." You cannot speak in two languages at once. Speak out in those funny sounding syllables. That is the beginning of your prayer language. Do not stop. Once a sound or syllable has come out, speak another one. Some people speak a rather fluent language right from the start. If they have been excited about this and they have a positive attitude, they will receive easily and speak out for awhile. If I am one of those people who ministers the baptism to people, I keep my eyes open and upon the candidate to see if he is shaking his head "no." Many people do that. If that is the case, I stop them and have them open their eyes and listen to me as I tell them they were shaking their head "no." I tell them to thank God and believe that they will receive. Then we go back to receiving.

In most cases, people will receive their prayer language here even though it sounds so foreign to them. If a person is struggling, sometimes I have all of us around the candidate to start praying out loud in our tongues and as the chatter around him grows, he does not feel so much pressure, or embarrassment, on him and he can quietly utter a few syllables or words in tongues.

Can a person receive by themselves? Certainly, many people do, sometimes when they were not even expecting it. I got it easily by myself. I just got by myself, without any instructions or anyone around, and I knew that I had to open my mouth and say something, so I thanked God and as I still had my eyes shut, I began to speak these "words" that seemed like warm oil coming out of my mouth. They flowed easily and beautifully. I spoke for three or four minutes, then I just basked in it.

But then, something happened that happens to most of the people who get it. I heard a voice that I thought was God because the voice said something like, "Now that you have this, you can see that it is not what you thought, so do not worry about this anymore and I will give you better things than this." The voice seemed to take credit for what happened so I assumed it was God. It was over four years later that I learned from a good brother that it was Satan and he does that every time a person gets the baptism. He lies to them. He usually says, from all of the people that have told me over the years, that "You just made that up. That wasn't God at all." I believe 80 to 90% of the people who receive a language will hear Satan try to lie to them and talk them out of it. It is almost always within the first few minutes after, to the first 24 hours or so. We always warn people that after they get it, they probably will be lied to by Satan. That is why I keep telling people that Satan hates the baptism of the Spirit more than salvation. I do not hear of near as many people who say that Satan lied to them about their salvation.

So, how do you get it by yourself? It is about the same steps as receiving with others around you. But the laying on of hands does help. It seems to strengthen the power coming down from the Lord.

Often it is easier to receive by yourself. You can get away by yourself to pray for this. Do the same as what I said earlier. Know that you are going to get this. It is not difficult. Quiet yourself and thank God for giving you the Holy Spirit and when you sense the Spirit come down upon you, open your mouth to speak out the first sound or syllable, then add more sounds as they come. Keep speaking for the more you speak, the more confidence you will gain as the words keep coming.

It may sound like I am putting a lot of emphasis on tongues. In a way I am, because tongues are the gateway to the Holy Spirit in this case. Tongues are the entry into the baptism. Many people ask if they can receive the baptism without tongues. Then, let me ask you, "Why would you want to try to do something different than what God ordained?" Why would you want to go against all of the examples found in the Book of Acts? Not only does the Bible show that tongues were involved in everyone who received, no exceptions, but my observation of all the people who have received, tells me that the Bible is very correct in showing tongues to be the evidence. I have heard many Christians say that they prayed for it and believed that they got it, but they did not speak out in tongues. They felt "warmth" as many do, some felt "light come down on them" and some felt "something like electricity." No matter what they felt, if they did not receive their prayer language, they showed no further proof that they received the baptism. Those who never spoke, never show any evidence of receiving, as opposed to the people who do receive the legitimate way. Those who get it "without tongues" are being deceived. They never go into the gifts of the Spirit, which often happens after a person gets it with his prayer language. There are signs of a person who receives. His love for Jesus greatly enlarges and his joy and faith increase several times over. Those of us who have received notice that we talk about Jesus much more than we did when we were Christians without the baptism and we also notice that when a new person receives they begin using the name of Jesus much more too. They begin to see the Bible in a more powerful, clear way. They will love people more. Many changes come with the baptism. They may not be as dramatic as mine, but they will come.

What if a person gets a sound and that is all, but he keeps repeating it in faith that he will get more? Until a person begins to get some words, he will be like a person who comes up to a locked door of a house that has a small broken pane of glass and he sticks his arm through the broken pane and waves his arm around claiming that he is in the house. Is he in the house? No, his arm is, but he is not. A person who gets at least a little bit of a language will be able to enter. However, they need to be shown how to enlarge their language so that they can freely communicate with the Lord. The baptism is all about a new, free, supernatural way to communicate with the Lord and with the spirit world so that we can have power to be witnesses for Jesus.

I have talked with several people who prayed for the baptism and "thought" they had it and lived that way for some years, but later prayed again and received it with tongues and they tell me that they saw a huge difference. They realized that they did not get it at first, like they thought, but when they got their prayer language, it changed things for them completely.

If you have trouble speaking a beginning of a language, after you have prayed, with or without other people, it is best to not struggle any more and just go somewhere by yourself and worship the Lord and stay in a positive attitude. If you are seeking that bad, you will receive.

I want to say a few things about expanding your language also. If you prayed and received only a few syllables or words, and that is all you have, don't worry, you can go on. You can pray now in the Spirit and begin to shape other words. You can do that. It is not you "making it up." It is God helping you to expand your communication with him. Every time you pray, you never know the first word or sound you are going to make. It is God every time. Tell your mind to be quiet and allow your spirit to take over, as is always in every case. Trouble comes when you try to figure out how to pray. It is not a mind thing, it is a spirit thing. I go for walks a lot, praying in the Spirit and thinking about something else a lot. I sometimes read the road signs while I am praying in the Spirit. I make plans and think about what I am going to be doing, all the while I am praying in the Spirit. If you have read the book this far, you are hungry enough to receive.

I want to close this chapter on why people do not receive the baptism of the Spirit. Several months ago my sister-in-law asked me, "Don, if the baptism of the Spirit is so wonderful, why doesn't everybody have it?" I asked her, "If Jesus really is the Savior and the Christian life is so wonderful, why are not most people saved?" She saw the point. I said the real reason is that most people are not ready to pay the price. Every time you go forward spiritually, you have to pay a price, and the deeper you want to go, the higher the price. Many pastors will be kicked out of their church if they tell them that they are baptized in the Spirit. Many Christians will be shunned and pushed out of their church if they receive. People can see that so they are not looking for the baptism of the Spirit. They prefer to keep their dignity and status.

However, I have observed that there are basically three reasons why Christians do not receive the baptism. The greatest reason, by far, is fear. Their fear of it may come from many places, but the biggest cause of that fear is the churches who teach that it is not for today, or it is of the devil or only those weird people do that, and a couple dozen other reasons. The ones who should be teaching truth and life and freedom are preaching fear and bondage, and I am talking about too many so called gospel churches. There are more lies about the baptism of the Holy Spirit than any other doctrine. After I had received, it occurred to me that everything I had heard about it was not true. Yes, it is fear, that comes directly from Satan, who keeps many people from getting it. Some are afraid of what their church would think, or their family would think, or something else. They choose to serve a denomination, or a creed, rather than the Living God. Their heart tugs at them, but they push back because they are afraid. I know Christians who have desired the baptism for forty years or more and yet they will not receive because they are so afraid of their church. Fear can keep you from so many wonderful blessings and the Holy Spirit is one.

The second biggest reason, and this is my observation, is ignorance. People are ignorant of the ways of the Holy Spirit. Paul said six times in the New Testament that he did not want his readers to be ignorant about something, so he would go ahead and teach them about a subject, such as the resurrection, in I Cor. 15:34. He told them that they should be ashamed for not knowing about the truth of the resurrection. Paul told the people he did not want them to be ignorant of the spiritual gifts in I Cor. 12:1. Too many Christians have never felt God's anointing and don't even know what it is. They have never seen anyone healed. They have never heard God speak to them. They have never seen a miracle. They have never been where there was powerful worship in the Spirit. They don't even know they have a spirit inside. They serve God in their soul. Most of this is the fault of the church, although a person is still responsible for their own learning.

The third reason that people do not receive the baptism is pride. Ouch, that hurt. But it's true. Know this for sure: spiritual pride is a powerful force in the lives of those who carry it. Pride keeps people from so many good things. It is particularly difficult for a pastor to admit that he does not know some simple spiritual teachings. He is the hardest to "unlearn" and then learn the things of God. All pride has to do is give in and humble himself before God and he will disappear and great things will start to enter in to replace the coldness and arrogance.

Don't be afraid, or ignorant, or proud. Receive.

CHAPTER 6

That powerful thing called your "spirit"

Most of the people in this world have no idea what they are missing by not coming to know Jesus as their Lord. Knowing that your sins are forgiven and the peace that follows is beyond words. It is the peace that passes all understanding. Phil. 4:7. Knowing where you are going after death is also a great strength. Being led of the Holy Spirit is also a lifestyle that cannot be surpassed, although not many Christians have reached that point yet. The Holy Spirit is a huge division, not because God wants it that way, but because many Christians do not know anything about it, or they think they know about it and have chosen not to pursue any further, and then there are those believers who wanted to go on in their spiritual lives and chose to find the fullness of the Holy Spirit and all that it includes.

For those of you who are Christians but have not experienced the baptism of the Spirit yet, and for those of you who have experienced it but with not much impact on your life, this chapter may not mean a great deal to you.

Even after reading this chapter, you still may not understand much about your spirit because your spirit only comes alive when it has been deeply invaded by the Holy Spirit, which is often at the time a person is baptized in the Spirit. When we are born again our spirit is made alive (Rom. 8:10), but as we have seen from the Book of Acts, the apostles wanted more than that and encouraged all believers to receive the baptism of the Spirit. They knew that God wanted our spirits opened up to the maximum so that we could hear God and truly be led of the Spirit, which is the Lord's perfect will for us. This chapter is about our spirit and some of the truths that can help us to be in tune with God.

First of all, we need to identify our spirit. What are we talking about when we say "our spirit?" It is best to start with some Bible definitions. It says in I Thess. 5:23: "May your whole spirit, soul and body be kept blameless at the coming of our Lord Jesus Christ." The Bible shows that we have 3 spiritual divisions: spirit, soul, and body. Though some people think that the spirit and soul are the same, they are actually very different. In Heb. 4:12 it says, "For the word of God is living and active. Sharper than any double-edged sword, it penetrates even to dividing soul and spirit, joints and marrow; it judges the thoughts and attitudes of the heart." We see here that the word of God can divide the soul and spirit, which means that the word can help us to see the difference between the two. Science, philosophy, and reason cannot explain the spirit. Unfortunately, many pastors can't either. However, the spirit and soul are two different things and they serve two different purposes. They cannot cross into the territory of the other even though they work together to make up a human being, especially a Christian.

The soul is our personality, our being that we project to others. It is our mind with all of its joys and fears. A soul implies a life, a living being. We are not rocks; we are souls. The soul of a person is where decisions are made, where memories hide, where sin takes place. Our soul is our human, frail, finite side.

Our spirit is the part of us that connects with God. It is another mind, the one that hears God and communicates with him. Yes, we have two minds, one in our soul (our brain), and one in our spirit. Have you ever found yourself arguing with yourself? Usually that is your spirit, where your conscience is, debating with the weaknesses of your soul, or flesh, as we sometime call it. The flesh and Spirit fight all the time. The Bible says that our spirit became spiritually alive when we became believers. The switch was turned on, however many Christians have not yet plugged into it. The baptism of the Spirit really wakes up your spirit and that is when many Christians first start finding this new treasure – their spirit. They begin to "hear" God and get a clearer direction in the things of their lives. They may receive prophecies, and if they do, it will be through their spirits, not their minds or souls. We receive all spiritual directions and revelation through our spirit. Satan speaks to our mind and God speaks to our spirit. The Bible clearly shows that our spirit is a separate receptor apart from the brain and the spirit is far greater in capacity than our little brain. Our spirit is almost limitless. Paul asks in I Cor. 2:11: "For who among men knows the thoughts of a man except the man's spirit within him?" Paul also said that he prays with his understanding (his mind) and he prays with his spirit (not using his mind but going through his spirit only). Paul would sing with his mind but also sing with his spirit. I Cor. 14:15. Your spirit is independent of your mind, has far greater capacity, and does not contain the elements of aging, dying, sickness, hopelessness, etc. These latter things are in your soul. In Mk. 2:8 Jesus had just forgiven the sins of the paralytic who was brought to him for healing and the teachers of the law were thinking that this was blasphemy. It says that, "Immediately Jesus knew in his spirit that this was what they were thinking." Jesus knew what they were thinking. How? By his spirit. Jesus operated in his spirit all of the time. Paul learned how to do that too and has tried to teach us that in much of his writings. It is the norm for the Christian, not the exception. Paul says that he serves God with his "whole heart" (NIV) but it literally is "spirit." Paul was led of the Holy Spirit speaking to his spirit as to where he should preach, who he should speak to, as to what person was receptive, who had demons and what the demons did, who was ready for healing and many other things, all by his spirit. We should do the same. It is the only way to truly be effective for the gospel.

Reader, you need to know that if you really want God's power in your life, you need to learn about the Holy Spirit and your spirit and how they work. You cannot operate in the soul realm and accomplish much in the Lord. You do not get a word of knowledge from your mind or soul. You get it through your spirit. None of the gifts of the Spirit operate through your mind. When you were saved you believed in your heart, which is another word for spirit. Faith operates in your spirit. You do not believe with your head. Many people unfortunately think that "believing in your heart" is purely a figure of speech, but no, it is literal. Far too many words, phrases, and verses have been dumped in the trash pile by calling them figures of speech. God's word is much more literal than you think. It says in Pro. 20:27 that "The lamp of the Lord searches the spirit of a man; it searches out his inmost being." What is the Lord searching for? Faith. Where is it found? In our spirit. All successes come from the spirit. Most disappointments and failures come through the soul, the mind, the feelings – those very fragile, man-made plans that crumble.

To show you even a more powerful proof of this, read the story of Elisha in II Kgs. 5. He had healed Naaman of leprosy who was a general in the army of the Arameans. Naaman offered Elisha many rich gifts for the deed but Elisha refused. After Naaman left, the servant of Elisha, Gehazi, slipped away to Naaman and made up a story that Elisha had changed his mind and needed some of the gifts. Naaman responded with lots of gifts. So he got back home with a load of goods and was met by Elisha, who asked him where he had been. Like an ornery child he blurted, "No where." Elisha quickly replied, "Was not my spirit with you when the man got down from his chariot to meet you?" He then told more of the scene and rebuked his servant sharply and said that he would receive Naaman's leprosy, which he did. But my point is that Elisha said that his spirit was observing Gehazi while he was sinning. Is that just a figure of speech? No, Elisha's spirit was able to travel and perform God's work. In some cases our spirit can travel and do the work of God. Paul's spirit was caught up to heaven for a time and witnessed amazing things. II Cor. 12. That can happen to believers. Our spirit can operate in many supernatural ways that our body and soul cannot. This is not hocus pocus or New Age theology. It is Biblical and real.

About 40 years ago, during the most supernatural night of my life, God was moving mightily and was talking to me for a long time, while doing some other things. He basically was teaching me and showing me things about him. He asked me, "Son, what is the greatest thing on earth?" All I could say was, "I don't know Father; you know." Then he replied, "It is your spirit." He further explained, "Your spirit has the capacity to memorize all of the Bible translations in English. Your spirit knows the number of carpet strands in your house. Your spirit knows this and much more. Your spirit knows ahead of time many things that your mind does not know yet." There were other things that he told me, but I remember that part the most.

If you are really interested in learning more about your spirit, go find a complete Bible concordance, if you know what that is, and look up the word "spirit." Some of the references are about the Holy Spirit, some are about evil spirits, and some are about the human spirit. Separate the uses and start looking and reading the passages about our spirit. Take notes on them and look it over. You will discover many new things. Also, if you want to learn more, find some people who are baptized in the Spirit and talk to them about these things. Don't spend years searching. You either believe or you don't.

I have run into many people who meet me and want to ask questions about spiritual things. It does not take too long to see if they are a true seeker or an "arguer." Is that a word? Those who are Billie Goat Christians, who are always saying, "Yeh but, yeh but," never find it. I hope you are serious, because there are great things for those who keep chasing God.

People often ask, "How do you learn to hear God and follow him in your spirit?" I always tell them to make sure that they have been born again and not just churchified. Then they need to get hungry enough for the Lord that they will want to be baptized in the Holy Spirit as described in the earlier part of this book. You cannot skip this part and expect to see much of the power of God, although there are a few exceptions to that. God will honor whatever faith you have. There are many people who have seen a miracle in their lives or a miraculous healing without experiencing the baptism of the Spirit, but again I say, these are more of the exception than the norm. For me, I want all of the Lord that he will give me and not a little bit less than that.

So if you receive the baptism, you took the first step of getting into deeper things than before. Once you receive you should start expanding your prayer language so that your praying in the spirit will be fluent. Then you ask God to help you receive whichever gifts he has for you. Study those because the more you know, the more you may be able to experience. Seek the Lord, not for experiences but to become the person that God wants you to become. It is too easy to work hard at doing the things of God, but he is calling us to "become" more and to "do" less.

Then, as you may start to be led more of the Spirit, you will begin to recognize his voice. Jesus promised us that his sheep would hear, or recognize, his voice. Jn. 10:4, 16. Get that deep into your spirit. When God speaks to you, it is different than a thought. It is clearer, more emphatic, more of a knowing. We know in our spirit, but guess in our mind. Our spirit is deeper. You will be able to tell the difference between your thoughts and God's voice. It does take practice and you probably will make a mistake. We all have, but get up and go on. I have witnessed many beginners who gave their first message in tongues at church, or prophecy, or word of knowledge. They were scared of making a mistake, so they held back. I have gone to them because God told me that they had a message at that time. As I told them, it confirmed to them that God was speaking to them. It gave them courage to speak it out next time. There is no sure, mathematical way to do this. You just keep stepping out in faith. Do not let fear of a mistake keep you from going on. The group that you are in will encourage you and help you. If you are in a non-Spirit-filled church, then you ought to consider looking up a prayer meeting or another group of people outside your church and fellowshipping while you are still going to your church. I am not advocating leaving your church, but maybe having two groups of people that you fellowship with. No matter how tempted you are to stay in the middle of your non-Spirit-filled church, you will never grow much in the things of the Spirit. I have seen many people receive the Holy Spirit and stay completely in their church and almost always die in the Spirit. They give up the deeper things and go back to the elemental things. The Galatians did this and Paul wrote most of his letter addressing it. See Gal. 1:6; 2:20; 3:1-5; 4:8, 9; 5:1, 16-18, 25; 6:8. I meet very few Christians who understand much about their spirit and you can see it in their lives. They are very limited to say the least. But I also meet some who are growing in their spirit and you can tell a difference. They are more excited, they talk about it, they experience Jesus more fully, and they have spiritual things to share. You can see the life of God in them, even though you may not know at first what it is. God desires that for you too. Open up your spirit. The more you desire God, the more he will give you and eventually he will begin to do things in your spirit and you will see the difference between your mind and your spirit.

CHAPTER 7

The gifts of the Spirit

Right after a person receives the baptism of the Spirit is a very good time for them to start looking into the possible next step – the gifts of the Spirit. In fact, I have noticed over the many years that once a person receives the baptism of the Spirit, they need to be instructed on the gifts and how to receive them, because if they have not received any gifts 8 or 10 months later, they probably will not receive any later. You should be hungry enough in the first few months of the new Spirit-filled experience that you will go after more of God and the gifts of the Spirit are the most obvious things that should follow. In other words, while the Spirit is still fresh upon you is the best time to go on and receive your gift or gifts. Far too many people get baptized in the Spirit and use it and are blessed by it, but as time goes on they lose the original anointing and although their life is a good level higher than before, they begin to level off and maybe even drift down somewhat. The baptism is no guarantee of a permanent, higher life. Just like salvation does not quickly and automatically make you mature in the Lord, it simply gives you the potential for all of that. The baptism does the same; it now gives you even more potential but it must be used and experienced as you follow the Lord. All gifts from God are "muscles." They must be used in order for you to grow.

Before I define and say a few things about each gift, I want to point out some things for searching people to know about them.

1. First, it is important to know that these are gifts "of the Spirit" or "from the Spirit." They are not learned, obtained in a Bible college, given by a denomination, or figured out and finally obtained by some human knowledge. They are given by God alone.

2. God gives the gifts to those whom he knows are spiritually fitted to use them, not the "most spiritual" necessarily, but to those who are ready and are called to do that particular work. A gift may evolve into a ministry and often does. The gifts of healing often lead that person into the healing ministry or a gift of discerning of spirits can lead into a ministry of deliverance. But the point is that these are "gifts" or free blessings from the Lord, given to people chosen by him.

3. The gifts most often follow the baptism of the Spirit, not before. See Acts 2:4. There is an exception occasionally, but you are probably not the exception. In my 40 years of this, the pattern has been, first the baptism of the Spirit, then the gifts. One Baptist evangelist that I was talking to said that he had a gift of healing, but when he received the baptism, the gift of healing greatly increased in power and other gifts came also. Funny isn't it? He was a Baptist but when the got the baptism,

he could no longer be a Baptist. Getting licensed to a denomination is like getting a driver's license for your city only. You can drive around in the city all you want, but you can't go anywhere else. I'm sorry. Let's go on.

4. These gifts come from seeking usually. Salvation came through seeking and all the steps in a Christian's life come through seeking. Ask, seek, find. They are not dropped on you as you are walking down the street. You will receive as much as you desire from God, but not more.

5. The gifts are given for others' sake, not your sake primarily. They are to build up the body of Christ and are sometimes used to win people to the body of Christ. Do not become so engrossed in "your" gift that you lose some of the effectiveness within the body.

6. These gifts are only temporary and spontaneous in nature and are not permanently in use at all times. It is God who chooses who and where and how long a gift will operate. I can sense the Spirit of prophecy upon me for a few hours at a time, and even when it leaves, I can still sense the power of God nearby, ready to fall again. Then sometimes a prophecy will come in church, I give it, then the Spirit lifts, at least from prophesying and I go on to other things as the Spirit leads. As a pastor, the Spirit is upon me most or all of the church service, but the Spirit falls upon me to prophesy, or give a word of knowledge or just to teach and I can easily feel God's anointing in all of the operations. I am not trying to impress you, but trying to tell you how it can be. Getting back to the temporariness of the gifts, you need to know that the gift of wisdom, for example, does not make you wiser. I hear and read comments like this all the time that Pastor so and so must have the gift of

wisdom because he is so wise and smart. This is plainly a lack of teaching in the church.

The gift of healing, though, may be a little different. That gift can often stay upon a person more permanently than the other gifts and when a person with the gift is called upon to pray for a healing, it may happen much or most of the time. I have heard Kathryn Kuhlman and Oral Roberts both say that the gift stays with them often but can sometimes not be so strong.

So much for the above. On the gifts, we can understand a little more before we go to definitions. It is interesting that as there are 9 fruit of the Spirit listed in Gal. 5:22, 23, there are also 9 gifts of the Spirit listed in I Cor. 12:8-10. It has been suggested that by this we ought to see that fruit in a Christian is every bit as important as the gifts. Fruit is actually more important. It is what we are to watch for toward those who call themselves prophets or even believers. See Mt. 7:15-23; Heb. 13:7. A Christian can be giftless but he cannot be fruitless. Tis better to have both.

The 9 gifts are often divided into 3 groups of 3 gifts each. There are the 3 gifts of revelation (the power to know) and they are the message of wisdom, the message of knowledge, and the discerning of spirits. Then there are the 3 gifts of power (the power to do) and they are the gift of faith, the gifts of healing, and the gift of miraculous powers. There are 3 gifts of utterance (the power to speak) and they include the gift of prophecy, the gift of tongues and the gift of interpretation of tongues.

So let's go over each gift and maybe say a few things about it. This is to help keep you on track and make sure you are reaching for the correct thing. At this point I want to thank a friend of mine, Pastor Roger Welty, for first coming up with these definitions. I have used his descriptions with a few changes.

The message of wisdom

The gift of the "message of wisdom" is listed first. More often, especially from the old timers and the King James Version it is called the "word of wisdom." When God speaks through someone with this gift, it is to reveal his purposes and instructions. They are known only to him and it is about a situation in the present or future. Kenneth Copeland calls it "God's shortcuts." It is usually a short word or message, perhaps a sentence or two and the simplicity of it is usually astonishing. One of the best examples of this is in the Old Testament where we do not think of the gifts of the Spirit, but it seemed to work like it. It was when 2 women were fighting over a child, both claiming it to be theirs and they brought the situation to Solomon. He commanded the child to be cut in two and a half given to each woman. Immediately the real mother screamed out to give the child to the other woman. Solomon knew that the real mother would do that. The gift works that way.

The message of knowledge

The gift of the "message of knowledge" is the second gift listed. It is a fragment of knowledge from God regarding facts about a situation unknown by any of man's ways. One of its most common uses is with the gift of healing. For example, God may use someone in church to stand up (at the right time) and give a message of knowledge and it is about someone there who has a bad heart and God wants to heal them. It just happens that a man is visiting that church and does not know anyone there. It is him and the sickness or medical problem is described exactly. That gift stirs up faith in the man and they are able to pray for him and see him healed. This is common in churches today that are open to God's ways. Often a person who has a gift of healing will also have a gift of the message of knowledge.

The gift of faith

The third gift named is the gift of faith. This is a supernatural impartation from God producing unwavering confidence to call for and/or receive the intervention of God in a situation. In other words this is an extra shot of faith put there by God himself so that a particular work gets done. This is beyond our normal faith that we should be using every day. The gift of faith and the gift of miracles sometimes work in conjunction with each other.

The gifts of healing

The gifts of healing are mentioned next. Notice the plural "gifts." There are different kinds or groups of sicknesses to be healed and people have different callings and gifts sometimes to heal particular diseases or pains. These gifts are supernatural empowerments to heal diseases or pains or injuries either instantaneously or by reversing the health problem, or sometimes the healing may start at that moment but take a certain time to finish. We often classify an instant healing as a miracle, more than a healing.

The gift of miraculous powers

The next gift is the gift of miraculous powers, or commonly called gift of miracles. It is the supernatural application of God's power to bring about manifestations of that which is outside the boundaries of natural, physical laws and their limitations. It is literally the "working of powers" or "working of miracles." This gift, like healing, has many avenues in which to work as shown by the plural.

The gift of prophecy

The gift of prophecy is supernatural utterance given by the Holy Spirit revealing his viewpoint, will and intentions in light of present and future earthly circumstances. Sometimes it is a teaching prophecy or just one that encourages or one that glorifies God as its main purpose. See I Cor. 14:3. A prophecy can give almost any kind of message and most of them have little to do with the future, though some do. Simply because someone has this gift does not make them a prophet. Prophets are still around as are all of the 5 main ministries in Eph. 4:11. A prophet tends to give longer, more detailed messages and more often is directed toward the future. Kenneth Hagin, himself a recognized prophet in the body of Christ, said that a prophet should have the 3 gifts of prophecy, knowledge, and discernment. Often a church may have 2 or 3 people with the gift of prophecy and all of them give more general words, shorter messages and not much about the future, as do people who prophesy but are not prophets.

Prophecy is not "anointed preaching" as several unlearned teachers may try to tell you. Some translations or paraphrases of the Bible use this term instead of the correct one. Calling it anointed preaching shows the ignorance and denial of teachers and translators. Nor is it someone who raises their voice and gets excited while preaching or teaching. It has nothing to do with volume or feelings. When I help people learn about the gifts, I stress that they give their messages, whether tongues, interpretation, prophecies, etc., in a clear, audible voice so that all can hear and understand. Some people think they have to shout or cry or sob their message, but this should be corrected for the good of the group.

The gift of distinguishing between spirits

The gift of distinguishing between spirits is the God-given ability to distinguish between spirits (good and evil) and also to know what kind of evil spirit it is, and to accurately know their activities with the end purpose of casting out the evil spirit, or demon or demons. Sometimes along with the gift, God will reveal where the evil came in, who the leader demon is, and how they are working together. Usually God will give the name of each demon. This information is beneficial to the person who has had the demons because it will help them in their future walk with the Lord. There is a great deal of teaching about demons and deliverance, but I won't give it here and get off the purpose of this book. If you want more information about demons and deliverance, I have written a paper on it, at this time. Let me know if you want a copy and I can get you one. See details at the end of this book.

The gift of tongues

The eighth gift mentioned is the gift of tongues. It is a language of men or angels given by the Spirit of God that is unknown to the speaker and is meant to be given to a group, small or large, with the purpose of having the gift of interpretation of tongues to follow, either by the speaker, or another person. This should not be mixed up with the tongues that people receive at the baptism of the Spirit. That is the evidence of the baptism of the Spirit. That experience is for all believers if they want to receive, but this gift that Paul is listing is for only some of the believers, only those whom God chooses. Many charismatic or Pentecostal churches have many members who pray in tongues but only a few in each church has the gift of tongues. Unfortunately, many of those churches are not seeing the gifts operate as much as they used to.

The gift of interpretation of tongues

The gift of interpretation of tongues is the supernatural ability to interpret the message in tongues and usually does follow the first gift. It can be given by the person who gave the message in tongues, or it can be given by someone else in the group. Often 2 or 3 people may receive the interpretation and it will be the same message, but only 1 person needs to speak it out. Note that it is not translation, it is interpretation. That is why sometimes a rather long message in tongues can be followed by a rather short interpretation, and vice versa.

Remember, all of these gifts are supernatural and they operate through a person's spirit, not a person's mind. In all of these gifts the voice of God must be heard and it is heard in our spirit. It is wonderful but rare when you come across a church where the Holy Spirit is moving and the people have been taught the things of God and the various gifts are at work, all in harmony and all to the glory of God.

There is a great deal more than can be taught about the gifts, but that will come as you put your heart in a place to receive and learn by using them.

May God bless you mightily as you progress onward in the Name of Jesus Christ. May you find all of God's perfect will in your life and show much fruit for the kingdom of God.

If you are interested in my Bible commentary (incomplete but helpful), I have it typed out in about 275 pages, size 8 ½ by 11, but it would be sent on a CD or zip drive. It is sketchy in places but has a lot of insight into the Bible passages where the Holy Spirit, gifts, demons, and deliverance are mentioned with notes that most other commentaries avoid. It is indexed. It is $8.00 for the commentary plus the zip drive or CD.

As I mentioned in this writing, I also have a paper that I wrote on demons and deliverance. It has some good information on certain demons and their working. It is 10 pages long. I can send it to you, postpaid for $3.00.

If you need more information or help of any kind, you may contact me.

Don Hightower, 160 West Main St., Prairie City, IL 61470

Ph. 309-775-1003 sherry.hightower354@gmail.com

Printed in the United States
By Bookmasters